DEFENDING THE NATION

Defending the Nation

THE
CIA

John Hamilton
ABDO Publishing Company

visit us at
www.abdopublishing.com

Published by ABDO Publishing Company, 4940 Viking Drive, Edina, Minnesota 55435.
Copyright © 2007 by Abdo Consulting Group, Inc. International copyrights reserved in all
countries. No part of this book may be reproduced in any form without written permission from
the publisher. The Checkerboard Library™ is a trademark and logo of ABDO Publishing
Company.

Printed in the United States.

Cover Photos: front, Getty Images; back, U.S. Air Force
Interior Photos: AP Images pp. 10, 23, 26; Corbis pp. 1, 5, 9, 11, 15, 17, 18, 19, 20, 21, 24, 25,
    29; Getty Images pp. 13, 16, 27, 28

Series Coordinator: Megan M. Gunderson
Editors: Heidi M. Dahmes, Megan M. Gunderson
Art Direction & Cover Design: Neil Klinepier

Library of Congress Cataloging-in-Publication Data

Hamilton, John, 1959-
  The CIA / John Hamilton.
     p. cm. -- (Defending the nation)
  Includes index.
  ISBN-13: 978-1-59679-756-7
  ISBN-10: 1-59679-756-8
  1. United States. Central Intelligence Agency--Juvenile literature. I. Title II. Series: Hamilton,
John, 1959- . Defending the nation.

  UB251.U5H36 2007
  327.1273--dc22

                                                                        2005035425

Contents

The Central Intelligence Agency 4

Timeline 6

Fun Facts 7

History of the CIA 8

How Does the CIA Work? 10

Kinds of Intelligence 14

The Intelligence Cycle 16

CIA Headquarters 20

Jobs at the CIA 22

Organization 24

The Future of the CIA 28

Glossary 30

Web Sites 31

Index 32

The Central Intelligence Agency

The Central Intelligence Agency (CIA) is often cloaked in mystery. Some people think only spies work for the CIA. They picture spies hiding in shadowy places dressed in trench coats. And, they imagine them sending secret messages and using weapons and gadgets like James Bond. This is only partly true.

A large part of the CIA's job is spying. This is called **covert** intelligence gathering. When instructed by the president, the CIA performs covert actions. And recently, it has become active in the war against **terrorism**. But the CIA also does much more.

The CIA's mission is to collect information from foreign countries. It then evaluates that intelligence and puts it in a report. The report is given to the U.S. president and other government officials.

The CIA does not make laws or decide how to deal with foreign countries. Only the president and Congress can do that. So, they rely on the CIA to get the best and most correct information available. That way, they can make good decisions about U.S. foreign policy.

The CIA has used its emblem since 1950. The 16-point star symbolizes bringing intelligence from all over the world to a central point.

Timeline

1942 - In June, the Office of Strategic Services was founded.

1947 - Congress passed the National Security Act of 1947, which established the National Security Council and the Central Intelligence Agency.

1959 - Construction began on CIA headquarters in the Langley neighborhood of McLean, Virginia. It was completed in 1963.

1980 - Congress passed the Intelligence Oversight Act of 1980.

1991 - Construction was completed on a new headquarters building attached to the original structure.

1999 - CIA headquarters became known as the George Bush Center for Intelligence.

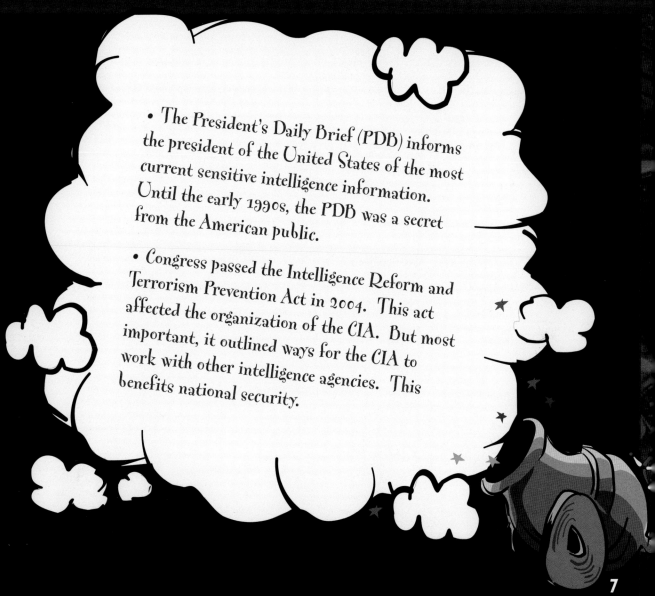

- The President's Daily Brief (PDB) informs the president of the United States of the most current sensitive intelligence information. Until the early 1990s, the PDB was a secret from the American public.

- Congress passed the Intelligence Reform and Terrorism Prevention Act in 2004. This act affected the organization of the CIA. But most important, it outlined ways for the CIA to work with other intelligence agencies. This benefits national security.

History of the CIA

The United States has used people to secretly collect information about its enemies since the **Revolutionary War**. Beginning in the 1880s, both the U.S. Army and the U.S. Navy had intelligence organizations. But, there was no coordinated government-wide intelligence organization until **World War II**.

In the late 1930s, President Franklin D. Roosevelt decided that the United States needed a more unified intelligence organization. This need became more pressing after the United States entered the war. So, the Office of Strategic Services (OSS) was founded in June 1942. The CIA has its roots in this early intelligence agency.

William J. "Wild Bill" Donovan organized and headed the OSS. Under his guidance, the agency gave the president secret information about the enemy. The OSS also conducted special operations, such as **sabotage**, against enemy forces. After World War II, the OSS was **disbanded**.

However, President Harry S. Truman recognized the need for continuing intelligence gathering in peacetime. So, Congress passed the National Security Act of 1947. The act established the National Security Council (NSC) and the CIA.

William J. Donovan

How Does the CIA Work?

By law, the president is the only person who can tell the CIA to carry out a mission. But, many things happen before the president calls on the CIA. First, the NSC **analyzes** secret information. Sometimes, it decides that **diplomacy** won't work or that military action is too extreme. Then, council members recommend to the president that the CIA begin a **covert** action.

If the president agrees with the NSC, he or she tells the CIA to perform a mission. CIA missions support U.S. foreign policy. But, there are times when the United States wants its activities to remain secret. So, many CIA missions are well hidden. And, they are not even publicly acknowledged by those in government.

A CIA covert action is different from intelligence gathering. Covert actions can include **propaganda**. This might involve distributing pamphlets with a certain viewpoint. Or, the CIA might

Each day, the CIA delivers the President's Daily Brief (PDB) in a leather binder.

have reporters include certain information in an article. **Covert** actions can also include supporting a particular political candidate in another country. But of course, these actions are all done secretly.

Providing up-to-date information to the right people helps the CIA work properly and successfully. Part of this involves distributing the PDB. This report provides the president and other top government officials with intelligence updates.

When the CIA began in 1947, many people thought it would rival the Soviet Union's intelligence agency, the KGB. The KGB was in charge of everything from intelligence to security. However, the CIA was to focus solely on foreign intelligence. So, it was normally forbidden by law from spying on U.S. citizens. This reassured U.S. citizens that the CIA would not conduct investigations against them.

Yet in the past, the CIA **abused** its power and spied on U.S. citizens. As a result, Congress passed the Intelligence Oversight Act of 1980. It required the CIA to report regularly to several oversight committees of the U.S. Congress. Oversight committees still authorize CIA programs and oversee their activities.

Today, the CIA is allowed to spy on U.S. citizens only under very special conditions. These include cases when international **terrorists** might be involved. However, the CIA mainly supports the fight against terrorism by collecting and **analyzing** information from foreign countries. The agency also works closely with friendly foreign governments and shares its **covert** intelligence with them.

Aldrich Ames was a CIA employee for 31 years. He was arrested in 1994 after the CIA discovered he was a double agent. He had been selling secrets to the KGB. Ames was sentenced to life imprisonment for his crimes.

Kinds of Intelligence

Intelligence can mean many things. Basically, it is information that the CIA collects. The U.S. government uses this intelligence to make decisions regarding foreign groups and governments.

There are several categories of intelligence. For example, current intelligence deals with day-to-day events. Estimative intelligence provides options for what may happen. And, warning intelligence alerts the government that a crisis could happen soon.

The CIA gathers intelligence in several ways. Collecting "open source" intelligence is most common. This type of information is available to anyone. It comes from sources such as newspapers or television broadcasts. The CIA also gathers human intelligence, or humint. This comes from human sources such as spies in a foreign group or country. These undercover missions can be very dangerous.

Imagery intelligence, or imint, comes from studying **satellite** images. The CIA also uses signals intelligence, or sigint. Sigint includes information from **nuclear**, **acoustic**, and **seismic** measurements. It also includes messages, such as radio signals or other communications, **intercepted** from foreign countries.

The CIA library contains more than 125,000 books and 1,700 periodicals, such as foreign newspapers. However, the library is only open to CIA employees.

The Intelligence Cycle

The CIA collects and **analyzes** information in a standard way. To do this, it uses a process called the intelligence cycle. This process helps ensure the CIA's job is done properly.

The intelligence cycle starts with a question from a policy maker. This may be the president or another government official. Once this specific information has been requested, the CIA begins the cycle.

First, the agency starts planning how best to obtain the requested information. The agency lists what it already knows and any questions it may have about the subject. Then, the CIA figures out how it will find the missing pieces of intelligence.

Next is the collection phase. The CIA gathers intelligence in several ways. Sometimes, information comes from

The United States has launched a variety of satellites into space. Some spy on other countries or listen to foreign communications. Others simply track weather patterns.

Satellites can reveal images of huge areas of land. Or, they can reveal photos so detailed they show city streets!

foreign newspapers. Other times, spies are sent into foreign countries. Often, the CIA also uses electronics and **satellite** photography to collect intelligence.

Once the raw information is collected, the CIA begins the next step in the intelligence cycle. The agency processes the intelligence gathered during the collection phase. A CIA member may write a description of a **satellite** photo. Or, someone may translate information from a foreign language into English. The processing stage makes complex information easier to understand.

Next is the **analysis** and production phase. At this time, CIA employees try to answer the original

2. Missing Pieces

1. Question

The Intelligence Cycle

6. Dissemination

question. They **analyze** and combine all the information the agency has gathered. Then, they write a final report with their conclusions and recommendations.

The dissemination phase is the last part of the intelligence cycle. The new intelligence is given, or disseminated, to whoever originally asked for it. Sometimes, new questions are asked because of a CIA report. In these cases, the whole intelligence cycle begins again.

3. Collection

4. Processing

5. Analysis and Production

CIA Headquarters

Soon after its founding, the CIA realized the need for a **secluded**, easily guarded place to work. But the agency also needed to be close to decision makers in Washington, D.C.

The Langley neighborhood of McLean, Virginia, was chosen as the perfect spot for the secretive agency's headquarters. Construction began in 1959 and was completed four years later.

Langley has been the CIA's home ever since. A new headquarters building connected to the original structure was completed in 1991.

CIA headquarters is extremely well protected. It sits on an approximately 250-acre (100-ha) site. Because of the need for secrecy and security, tours of CIA headquarters are not available to the public.

In 1999, the name of CIA headquarters changed to the George Bush Center for Intelligence. Former president George H.W.

Signs point to CIA headquarters. But, visitors are generally not allowed inside!

Bush was director of central intelligence from 1976 to 1977. He is the only director who went on to become president.

Inside the George Bush Center for Intelligence, there is a museum called the National Historical Collection. It holds many historical items, including spy gadgets such as miniature cameras. However, the museum is not open to the public.

CIA headquarters in Virginia

Jobs at the CIA

The exact number of people who work for the CIA is secret. For national security reasons, so is the agency's budget. The CIA is very careful about who it hires.

Applicants must be U.S. citizens who are at least 18 years old. Candidates must also be healthy and in good physical condition. A college degree is highly recommended, but not always required. The CIA considers other factors, such as life experience, when hiring employees.

A person hired by the CIA must also pass a background investigation. The CIA examines everything from a person's activities to his or her character.

Collecting **covert** intelligence for the CIA is a very demanding job. Spies must be smart, tough, and willing to work under hostile conditions. If they are captured, their lives may be in danger. But if they do their jobs well, they may collect information that will keep the United States safe.

Not all jobs at the CIA are for spies. In fact, the agency hires highly qualified people in a variety of professions. These include scientists, engineers, computer programmers, economists, mathematicians, and foreign language experts.

Just like at other government agencies, not all CIA employees are human! The CIA Canine Corps trains dogs for a variety of tasks, including sniffing out bombs.

Organization

The director of the Central Intelligence Agency heads the CIA. He or she manages all intelligence-gathering activities. The director also makes sure that intelligence is shared with all appropriate officials.

The CIA is divided into four teams called directorates. These are Operations, Science and Technology, Intelligence, and Support. The directorates help the agency collect and **analyze** information in the best way possible.

The Directorates of Operations and Science and Technology collect intelligence. The Directorate of Intelligence analyzes the information and writes conclusions about it for the president and other government officials. The

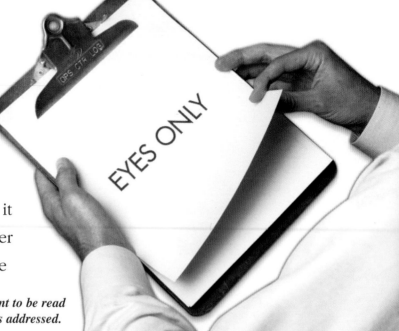

"Eyes only" information is meant to be read only by the person to whom it is addressed.

A memorial in CIA headquarters honors officers killed in service. Each star represents one officer. If an officer is still considered undercover, his or her name is not included.

Directorate of Support is there to make sure the other three teams can do their jobs smoothly.

The Directorate of Operations is the unit most often seen in movies and on television. Humint officers, or spies, work for the Directorate of Operations. They work undercover, secretly, and in foreign countries. In these ways, they collect information that might affect America's security.

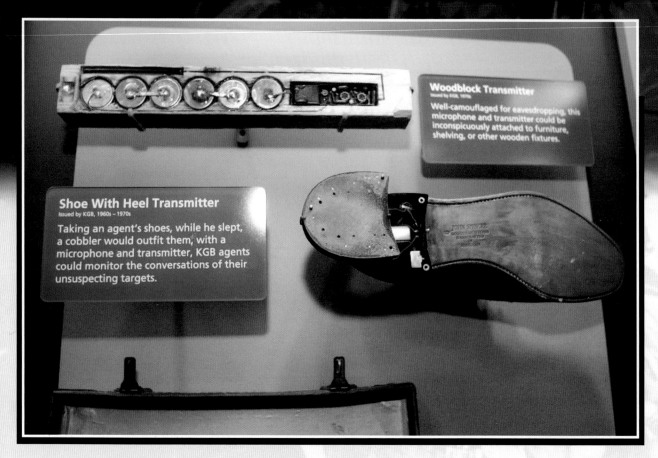

Woodblock Transmitter
Issued by KGB, 1970s

Well-camouflaged for eavesdropping, this microphone and transmitter could be inconspicuously attached to furniture, shelving, or other wooden fixtures.

Shoe With Heel Transmitter
Issued by KGB, 1960s – 1970s

Taking an agent's shoes, while he slept, a cobbler would outfit them, with a microphone and transmitter, KGB agents could monitor the conversations of their unsuspecting targets.

Another important part of the CIA is the Directorate of Science and Technology. It collects intelligence from television, newspapers, magazines, and radio. And, it **intercepts** secret messages from foreign groups and countries.

The Directorate of Science and Technology also keeps the agency up to date on modern technology. It is responsible for inventing and running technical operations. And, it works with the National **Reconnaissance** Office, which designs and operates spy **satellites**.

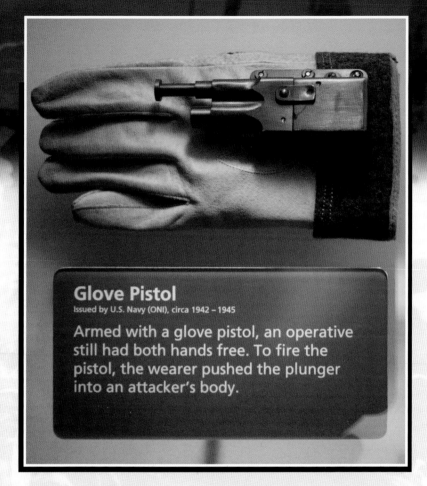

Glove Pistol
Issued by U.S. Navy (ONI), circa 1942 – 1945

Armed with a glove pistol, an operative still had both hands free. To fire the pistol, the wearer pushed the plunger into an attacker's body.

The Directorate of Science and Technology also designs new spy gadgets. Eventually, some of these tools may end up in the International Spy Museum in Washington, D.C. This museum houses gadgets from both the movies and real life.

The Directorate of Intelligence takes all the information gathered from a mission. It studies the raw data and tries to determine what foreign groups or countries are doing. Then, it makes a conclusion and writes a report. This report goes to the president or another appropriate official.

The Directorate of Support ensures that the other three teams have all the necessary tools and support. This unit provides security at CIA headquarters. And, it makes sure only the best people are hired to work for the CIA.

The Future of the CIA

On September 11, 2001, **terrorists** flew airplanes into New York City's World Trade Center buildings, destroying them both. Another plane was flown into the Pentagon. This is the U.S. Department of Defense headquarters in Washington, D.C. And, a fourth plane crashed in rural Pennsylvania.

Former congressman Porter J. Goss became director of central intelligence in 2004. After the Intelligence Reform and Terrorism Prevention Act of 2004, Goss's title became director of the Central Intelligence Agency.

On May 30, 2006, U.S. Air Force general Michael V. Hayden became director of the CIA.

The CIA and other government agencies were criticized for not preventing the attacks. So today, the CIA has shifted much of its focus to finding and stopping **terrorist** groups.

One group assigned to this duty is the CIA's Special Activities Division (SAD). This is one of the U.S. government's most secret groups. SAD officers are often retired men from the U.S. military. These men are highly skilled at using various weapons, aircraft, and intelligence tools.

Following the September 11 attacks, SAD teams helped the U.S. military identify targets and collect intelligence in Afghanistan. There, the CIA also used robotic Predator drones. These pilotless airplanes identify and destroy terrorist groups.

As the fight against terrorism continues, the CIA's job becomes increasingly important. Reliable intelligence and technology will help the U.S. government decide how best to respond to continuing threats. This will guarantee a safe and secure America for generations to come.

Glossary

abuse - to use incorrectly or improperly.

acoustic - of or relating to sound.

analyze - to determine the meaning of something by breaking down its parts.

covert (KOH-vuhrt) - kept secret, veiled, or concealed.

diplomacy - the practice of handling discussions and compromises between nations.

disband - to break up something that is organized.

intercept - to interrupt the progress of something before it arrives at its destination, usually secretly.

nuclear - of or relating to the energy created when atoms are divided or combined. An atomic bomb is a nuclear weapon.

propaganda - the spreading of ideas or information in order to promote or damage a cause, a person, or an institution.

reconnaissance (rih-KAH-nuh-zuhnts) - an inspection the military uses to gain information about enemy territory.

Revolutionary War - from 1775 to 1783. A war for independence between Great Britain and its North American colonies. The colonists won and created the United States of America.

sabotage (SA-buh-tahzh) - to damage or destroy something on purpose.
Sabotage is often carried out by a person who wants to harm an
enemy nation.

satellite - a manufactured object that orbits Earth.

seclude - to cut off from others.

seismic - of or relating to vibrations in the earth.

terrorism - the use of terror, violence, or threats to frighten people into
action. A person who commits an act of terrorism is called a terrorist.

World War II - from 1939 to 1945, fought in Europe, Asia, and Africa.
Great Britain, France, the United States, the Soviet Union, and their
allies were on one side. Germany, Italy, Japan, and their allies were
on the other side.

Web Sites

To learn more about the CIA, visit ABDO Publishing Company on the
World Wide Web at **www.abdopublishing.com**. Web sites about the
CIA are featured on our Book Links page. These links are routinely
monitored and updated to provide the most current information available.

Index

B

Bush, President George
H.W. 20, 21

C

Congress 4, 9, 12

covert intelligence 4, 8,
10, 11, 12, 22, 25

D

directorates 24, 25, 26, 27

Donovan, William J. 8

E

enemies 4, 8, 12, 28, 29

G

George Bush Center for
Intelligence 20, 21, 27

I

Intelligence Oversight Act
of 1980 12

K

KGB 12

N

National Historical
Collection 21

National Reconnaissance
Office 26

National Security Act of
1947 9

National Security Council
9, 10

O

Office of Strategic Services
8

P

propaganda 10, 11

R

Revolutionary War 8

Roosevelt, President
Franklin D. 8

S

sabotage 8

satellites 14, 17, 18, 26

September 11, 2001 28,
29

Special Activities Division
29

spying 4, 12, 14, 17, 21,
22, 23, 25, 26

T

Truman, President Harry S.
9

U

U.S. Army 8

U.S. Department of
Defense 28

U.S. Navy 8

U.S. president 4, 8, 10,
16, 20, 21, 24, 27

W

weapons 4, 29

World War II 8